Wholesome Nettle Content

❖ 13 Nettle Recipes for Hearth and Home ❖

By Kate Shaw

For Henry, Oscar, the half and quarter-lings;

If all we leave in our wake are the stories we founded during our time here, then we filled the days well and stocked the pantry of life with a bountiful harvest for those who wander our sacred home next.

Chapters -

- Foreword
1. Beverages
2. Sweet Treats
3. Main Dishes
4. Preservation
5. Note from the Author

Foreword

When it comes to beginning foraging, beyond it feeling mildly daunting, its practicality is easily questionable. While it's incredibly fun to head into nature and spy a coveted fungi or weed ripe for picking, it always begs the question – how will I cook this? And more importantly, will I even enjoy it?

I'm relatively new to the practise and put it forward to you, the lovely reader of this book, that there is a very real chance you already know more about foraging than I do. I don't and won't claim to be anything beyond a novice in this field. Thankfully I am guided by people more knowledgeable than myself. It's complete trust in their expertise that makes me feel confident in taking what we find on our woodland rambles into the kitchen. It's here I attempt to incorporate the abundance of free food into our daily meals, in a way that is realistic as well as nutritious.

While it is delightfully whimsical to follow a historical recipe, the reality is it's highly unlikely to filter into your everyday diet and become a reliable way to incorporate these incredible plants into your family's weekly meal plan. I write this very conscious of the timeline we live in; food prices are rising, the cost of living is ever on the up and we're becoming painfully aware of the ever widening abyss between the money we can bring home and the money we need to pay out in turn.

I believe it'll do us the world of good if we encourage each other to become more inventive in ways to keep ourselves and our folk healthy, well fed, and stronger than ever. We have a world of free nutrients quite literally at our feet, we'd be so foolish to continue cutting them back to make way for our neighbours' approval through manicured gardens.

The recipes in this book are tried and tested, some even by the pickiest of eaters known to mankind (aka, a very stubborn 6-year-old) and are firm favourites in our home.

I don't claim to be reinventing the wheel here, but the recipes are all also of my own creation or, as a gem to be found in the sweet treat chapter, a twist on a long-standing family favourite that spans not only generations but reaches the tips of my family tree. I may stand corrected, as the cheese rarely stands alone, but I don't believe you'll find these recipes – bar perhaps 'Nettle Tea' – replicated elsewhere online, so it is my most ardent wish you find the following useful and potential inspiration to get creative in your own kitchen.

While in this book I'll be focusing purely on the use of nettles, more information on the nutrition of nettles, their potential benefits as well as their historical significance can be found in my favourite human's book 'The Woodland Warrior' by Henry Dagger (Part 5: The Nutrition of the Woodland Warrior) also available on Kindle, who explains it all much better than I could.

And on that note, adventurous reader, I'll leave you in peace.

Beverages

This section is, as it stands, probably one for the grown-ups (unless you have an very adventurous child, the kind that takes to olives at a tapas restaurant aged 3 – however, my child feels exotic if we swap strawberry jam for raspberry in our sandwiches.) However, it contains the first way in which nettles were prepared for me, it feels as good a place to start as any as it firmly sits in my core memories. Nettles have quite a strong, almost earthy kind of taste. It's unlike any other flavour you're likely to have encountered before. Other plants you can forage to add to dishes tend to have a universal counterpart you can compare it to which instantly revokes a taste bud memory, like horseradish, lemon peel, or garlic. When it comes to nettles it's a struggle to find it a partner to give you an idea of what to expect beyond comparing it, in a stereotypical manner, to marmite. You will either love it instantly, hate it forever or maybe sit somewhere in the middle where the potential health benefits are enough to keep you at it. If your experience with nettles only goes as far as childhood stings, I'd suggest the first recipe being the best way to introduce your tastebuds to (what I think) is the tastiest culinary secret in England.

A SIMPLE NETTLE TEA

Nettle Tea

Ingredients: Fresh nettle shoots

Cold water

This is an easy one to eyeball measurements for. If common sense fails, a deeply rooted ancestral knowledge of 'that'll do' will waken in its stead. (I'd also suggest 2 – 3 plant tops per 1 mug of water is about right.)

Snip the freshest leaves and shoots at the top of the plant (I try to never take the plant lower than the first set of leaves below the shoot; see photo) directly into your container If you're feeling braver than I ever do, instructions on hand picking with minimal sting can be found in Woodland Warrior.

Return to the kitchen, quickly rinse the leaves under a running tap and place in your saucepan, adding enough water to cover the leaves.

Place on a very low heat for 15-20 minutes, avoid bringing to the boil.

Pour into mugs, straining the leaves, and enjoy.

Notes:

If the crop you've found have drooping seed pods, move to fresher pastures, or wait for the years second crop.

Leaves can be saved in the pan to use for a second tea, simply top up water levels and seep again on a low heat for 15-20 minutes.

The leaves, along with any water remaining, after the second cup can be added to your garden compost.

Tea is the most straight forward way to add nettles to your diet, although not the most fun. If you find you've taken to this method of preparation, details on how to preserve fresh nettle shoots for teas through the off season months are in the second to last section of this book.

Nettle Wine

Ingredients: 2 ltr jug filled with nettle shoots

4 tbsp ginger powder

1kg granulated sugar

4 ltr water

1 packet of general wine yeast

Method:

Add the nettle shoots, ginger and sugar to a large pan along with 2 litres of boiling water. Stir well to start dissolving the sugar and put on a low heat for 25 minutes. Remove from heat and pour the mixture into a sterilised fermentation bucket, adding another 2 litres of water and giving it a quick stir before sprinkling your wine yeast on top and sealing with a lid.

You want to leave the container in a warm place for 4 – 5 days, stirring daily, before straining the liquid away from the leaves and transferring to sterilised demijohn. Place the demijohn in a warm place until the airlock bubbler has either slowed or stopped producing bubbles completely, at this stage you can rack off the wine and enjoy. This is a very quick brewing wine, from picking to sipping in 5 months or so.

Note: We made our wine in Summer, around the time elderberries were ready to harvest, and enjoyed it through Autumn into early Spring. The flavour of the wine will depend on the freshness of the nettle tops themselves, although the tops will always be the freshest some home brewers prefer making their wine with the very first shoots of the year. But as much as it is to each their own, you may find yourself wanting to try making this wine later in the year. I can add from our experience, nettles harvested in early July make a delicate wine in their own right.

You can divide and multiply the ingredients as you wish, and I'm sure as the seasons repeat, you'll find your own sweet spot with measurements that work for you.

While you might feel the urge to buy the specialist equipment, the items needed for brewing can be found easily around your home, or cheaply if not. I know people who have brewed mead in cereal storage tubs, and I've personally had good luck using an empty 5ltr plastic water bottles as a makeshift demijohn. Not forgetting to save any wine bottles, especially those with screw tops, in the fermentation interim, The only thing I would recommend sourcing would be the bubble airlock, which can be found very cheaply in your average family run 'we sell everything' hardware shop, just to have an accurate gauge on the fermentation process. But if you feel thoroughly rebellious against the status quo, there are even ways to make your own using a balloon on online home brewers' forums.

Sweet Treats

Ask any long-suffering member of my family and they'll confirm the truth in this; my favourite place to hide nettles is in the sweetest of treats. While throwing 'nettle' into the name of any desert combination feels hopelessly romantic to me, anyone who hasn't become a fully paid-up member of the Nettle Supporters Party will arch their eyebrow in suspicion at whatever is placed before them.

The fantastic thing about nettles in cooking and baking is that, for the most part, despite their strong flavour when touted about solo you generally can't taste them out in other dishes unless you're *looking* for them. Being the little powerhouses of nutrients that they are, throw some nettle powder into your chocolate cake and it's basically transformed into a wholesome salad. 5 squares of fudge could well be your government mandated* fruit and vegetable portion covered, as through the power of just deciding something to be true; any and all things are possible.

In the next section I'm sharing what are my favourite nettle recipes . I make these so often that I'm beyond confident they will become favourites with your family too.

It's worth noting before we flit onwards that the recipes primarily use powdered nettles. This is something you can buy readily online, but is incredibly easy to make yourself. In the preservation section of this book I do lay out very simple instructions on how to preserve nettles for use year round, so don't feel as if you need to jump over to eBay and order a 50g packet just yet.

*suggested, but mandated sounds edgier and more punk to me.

SALTED NETTLE FUDGE

Nettle Fudge

Ingredients: 410g Evaporated Milk

525g Sugar

155g Butter

3-4 teaspoons of Nettle Powder

Vanilla Essence

A pinch of salt

Method:

Place a pan over a medium heat and add the evaporated milk, sugar and butter.

Stir gently while ingredients melt, once the grains of sugar have dissolved you can turn the heat up slighty and bring the mixture to a boil – keep stirring consistently, but there's no need to go at the pan like it insulted your Mother, we just don't want it to catch on the bottom of the pan.

Once the mixture has come to a boil, keep stirring slowly until the colour deepens to a glorious caramel shade and has thickened.

At this stage remove from the heat.

- A sugar thermometer should have hit around 118c
- A drop of the mixture into ice cold water should form a soft ball

Leave the fudge to cool for around 10 minutes.

Once it's cooled, transfer to a stand mixer and add the dash of vanilla, teaspoons of nettle powder and pinch of salt.

Beat for 5 minutes or until the fudge loses its glossiness and thickens. You can, of course, do this part by hand and sheer physical prowess. But I don't possess the latter, so my whisk armed robot does it for me.

Lastly, move the fudge to a square tin lined with greaseproof paper to set for around 3 hours. Slice into squares and enjoy!

Notes: If at any time the mixture burns, remove from heat and mix quickly to dissolve the brown pieces.

This is a universal fudge recipe with a few tweaks I've made over time to get the right consistency for how we like it – at this stage of the game you could honestly add whatever fluffs your imagination but here are my favourites:

- A dash of vanilla extract, 3 teaspoons of nettle powder and a generous pinch of salt.
- 4 teaspoons of nettle powder and a shot of rum.
- 2 teaspoons of nettle powder, 50g dark chocolate and zest of one orange.

If your fudge doesn't set, not all hope is lost. Simply return to the pan with half a mug of water and heat slowly to the boiling point again, incorporating the water into the fudge as it warms. Once you're back at the boiling point, keep a close eye as you stir and the water evaporates. All that's happened here is the fudge didn't quite reach the temperature it needed to. (It's happened to me many times and still does) Check the temp or do the ice water test before continuing the steps on cooling and beating the fudge. It'll submit eventually.

HIGHLANDER NETTLE SHORTBREAD

Nettle Shortbread

Ingredients: 1 tablespoon Nettle Powder

140g Salted Butter, cubed

200g Plain flour

80g Sugar

Demerara Sugar, for coating

Method:

Preheat your oven to 165c (fan assisted) and line 2 baking trays with greaseproof paper.

Cream the salted butter with the sugar until it's fluffy, adding in the flour, nettle powder, and mixing together to a rough dough.

Turn out onto a lightly floured surface and knead the dough until smooth.

Work the dough into a long sausage – aiming for about 2" in diameter – and wrap in cling film before chilling in the fridge for around 20 minutes until the dough has firmed.

Remove the questionable looking dough sausage from its casing and roll into the demerara sugar – it's easiest to place the sugar into a clean baking tray and roll the dough over.

Slice into ½ " thick circles and place onto the prepared trays.

Bake for 10-12 minutes or until the crumb has turned golden. Leave to cool for 5 minutes before transferring to a rack.

Family Lore.

Keep with me for a second as I channel the spirit of a food blogger describing the crisp Winter morning that inspired her to the kitchen, but this recipe warrants a little introduction. Every family member has a recipe. My Mum makes stew and dumplings that could have put King Harold over, my Dad is a dab hand at pancakes, my Sister makes earth shattering salted toffee biscuits and my Brother works small miracles with pork chops. The following recipe is my Grandma's through and through. One taste of the fudge filling and I'm hurtled backwards in time to her giant oak dining room table with my Sister on a Saturday. My Dad would be working for our family's builders yard, and my ever busy Mum took on extra shifts at  the chip shop, leaving us with my Grandparents for the day. My Grandmas home was built by my Grandad and has, for my whole life, been a place of orderly calm, with a lingering scent of pledge and a chocolatey treat waiting to be shared from an old Marks and Sparks shortbread tin. My beautiful Grandma still makes this cake every Christmas. One for my parents' home, and the other for my uncles. My Sister and I have both taken the recipe to heart, and I'm sure one day our children will be carrying the recipe onto their children and loved ones in turn. This, in a wildly over the top way, feels like part of my family story. I happily, and sometimes even without request, share the recipe freely to bring a little sweet slice of a warm Yorkshire home to whomever I can.

For where there is good cake, there is always good company.

Grandma Grindles Nettle Fudge Cake

Ingredients:

The weight of 4 eggs in their shell (typically 240g) in margarine, and sugar.

210g Self Raising Flour

30g Cocoa Powder

1 tbs of milk

1 tbs nettle powder

Method:

Preheat your oven to 140c (fan assisted)

Cream together the margarine and sugar until light and fluffy.

Add the 4 eggs, one at a time, with a tablespoon of flour, combining well after each egg.

Mix in the rest of the flour, cocoa powder, nettle powder and milk. Beat the mixture until everything is well combined.

Grease two cake tins with a little margarine and a light coating of flour. Divide the mixture evenly between both cake tins and bake, if possible, on the same oven shelf for 35 minutes. The cakes should be springy to the touch when they're done.

Remove from the oven and leave to cool in their tins for 5 minutes before moving to wire rack to cool completely. They will sink to level as they cool (see photo) but this means inside is a grand old fudgy chocolate sponge.

Once the cakes are cooled, we get to add the Grindle magic.

Fudge Filling

*A recipe so quintessentially vintage,
we're taking it back to ounce measurements.*

Ingredients:

8oz Icing Sugar

2 tbsp evaporated milk

2 oz Milk Chocolate
Grandma insists we use Cadbury's here

4oz Salted Butter

Method:

Mix 2 tablespoons of evaporated milk into the icing sugar. It'll come to a crumbly kind of consistency.

In a pan on the hob, melt your butter. Once the butter is melted remove from the heat and add in your squares of chocolate, mixing until they're melted and combined.

Pour the melted ingredients into the icing sugar, and mix. I won't kid you, it's going to look beyond questionable. A little gross. Suspiciously lumpy, infact. But keep mixing, soon the ingredients all join forces and you'll be staring into a bowl of smooth soft fudge filling.

Before the mixture starts setting you'll want to quickly spoon it onto the top of one of the cakes, smoothing out to the edges before sandwiching the other layer on top.

Leave the fudge to firm for around an hour, and you're all set. Quite literally!

While I've left this recipe in it's original state to honour my Grandma, it is free for some foraging foolery by the addition of nettle powder. You could also add orange zest to really kick it up a level. This cake is best enjoyed with a glass of milk or a strong coffee. My Sister's long standing tradition is to eat both layers of cake first, leaving the set fudge until last. As soon as you taste it, I'm pretty confident you'll understand why.

LEMON, DANDELION AND NETTLE CAKE

Lemon and Nettle Cake*
*the dandelion comes in the buttercream

Ingredients:

The weight of 4 eggs in their shell of sugar, margarine and self raising flour.

The zest of 2 lemons, and juice of 1

2 tbs Nettle Powder

Method:

Preheat the oven to 140c (fan assisted)

Cream butter and sugar together until perfectly fluffy.

Add the eggs one at a time, along with a tablespoon of self raising flour, combining well in between. After the last egg, fold in the rest of the flour along with the nettle powder and beat well.

Zest in 2 lemons and squeeze in the juice of one – you can use your hand to catch any kamikaze pips. Mix until evenly distributed.

Grease two cake tins with a little margarine and light coat of flour. Separate the mixture evenly between the tins.

Bake in the oven, on the same shelf if possible, for 35 minutes. The cake should bounce back if lightly pressed on the top.

Leave to cool in the tin for 5 minutes before transferring to a wire rack.

I like to layer the sponge with a generous amount of buttercream and lemon curd as a filling, and buttercream on top. Cake decorating is not my strong suit, so I just plop it on top and even it out claiming it's 'romantically rustic' and exactly how I intended it to look.

You can add an extra foraged treat here by using edible wild flowers on top. In the recipe photo I added primrose found on the walk to collect dandelions, nettles and wild garlic.

If you're unsure of a plants edibility, or aren't confident of an identification you've made, it's best to leave be. Nettles and Dandelions alone make this a little beauty of a foragers treat.

Lemon and Dandelion Buttercream

Ingredients:

200g unsalted butter, cubed at room temp

400g icing sugar

Zest and juice of 2 lemons

Yellow petals of 3 dandelion heads

Method:

In a large bowl cream the butter into the icing sugar. If you find the butter is still firm, you can place the bowl in the cooling oven to soften further.

Once smooth, add in the lemon zest and juice and beat until fluffy. The lemon juice will both lighten the buttercream slightly as well as deepening the lemon flavour.

Add the petals and stir to combine.

Nettle Chocolates

This recipe is a twist on Grandma's fudge filling

Ingredients: 8oz Icing Sugar

1 tbsp evaporated milk

2 oz Milk Chocolate

4oz Salted Butter

1 tbs Nettle Powder

200g dark chocolate

Method:

In a large bowl incorporate 1 tablespoon of evaporated milk with the icing sugar and nettle powder.

Melt the butter in a pan, once melted add in the chocolate and stir until melted and well incorporated. Add this into the icing sugar mixture, and beat until smooth and a fudge texture.

Using a little icing sugar on your fingers, roll a tea spoon of fool's fudge into a ball and place on a baking tray lined with greaseproof paper. You can, in all honesty, make these to whatever size you like.

While the fool's fudge sets, place the dark chocolate into a bowl and melt gently over a pan of simmering water.

In turn, I find a fork the best thing to use, lower the fudge balls into the chocolate to coat them. Once coated let any excess drip off and place back on the baking tray. Leave the chocolate to set and store in a tin, in a cool place, these should last several days but never make it that far in our home.

Note: If you're wanting to decorate the chocolates I'd suggest coating them in batches of 5 or so, and then you can add any toppings before they set.

Our favourites are;

- Pretzels
- Coarse salt
- Cocoa powder
- Candied fruit peel
- Sprinkles

Main Meals

There's a feeling of immense gratification that comes from seeing a table of empty plates following a meal you've lovingly put together for your family. Silence bar the sound of cutlery on plates (bar that spine-shattered screech, you'll know the one I mean) or polite questioning of if there's more food in the kitchen is better than the heartiest of 'thank you's in confirmation of a job well done. And knowing it has come off the back of a well balanced meal? All the sweeter.

One quick and easy way to incorporate nettles into your diet is to simply swap wilted spinach out of meals and throw in nettles instead – the cooking or blanching will remove the sting in the process – and you can't tell the difference. Or if you've prepared your nettles and have a hearty store of powder at hand, you can sprinkle it into most dishes for an added nutrient kick. It's not everyone's cup of tea, but I even like it as a topper to Greek yoghurt and honey.

I'm the happy mother of a rather picky eater who will happily add the powder to our Bolognese, much to my continued amazement. Tomato is very handy at covering the taste of nettles, and the dispersed powder in kids favourites such as tomato soup is akin to looking like pepper so it's incredibly easy to get into their diets under the radar too.

Due to it's immense sneak-a-bility from a family view point, I wholeheartedly encourage you to use your wits and steadily add powder to meals as you're cooking them, taste as you go and see. A little bit is better than none, and a whole lot is just peachy. On the next few pages are, again, my favourite recipes for tea time using nettles. I feel as if calling them my favourites rings a tad redundant, imagine if I were sharing the awful ones?

NETTLE PASTA

Nettle Pasta

Basic Ingredients: 1 egg

10g fresh nettles

100g flour

Method:

In a food processor, blitz the nettles into the powder. Once combined add the egg and process again until it comes together in a dough.

Once formed, tip out onto a well floured worktop and knead until smooth.

Wrap in clingfilm and rest for 30 minutes.

On a floured work surface, roll out the dough as thin as you can – I aim for a few millimetres – from here you can cut into long strips like tagliatelle or rectangles for lasagne.

Cook the pasta as fresh as you can in a pan of well salted boiling water for 3-4 minutes, drain and enjoy!

Notes:

The amounts of the recipe constitute the basic ratio. It's very simple to remember at 100, 10, 1 and this will make enough tagliatelle for two. Double quantities will make enough for a family lasagne. If it's your first time making pasta, just use the basic 1 egg ratio, and see how you go. Once you've got a feel for it you'll be able to multiply for your needs easily.

As this contains egg, if you're not planning to use it straight away once rolled make sure it's stored in the fridge and cooked within 24 hours.

I make this without a pasta roller, using my Grandma's old marble pastry rolling pin on a glass surface which works perfectly for me. While tempting to plump for a pasta roller, or to think you need fancy equipment to make something like pasta, it's more than possible to do it with things you already have in your kitchen and some added gusto – I am on my tip toes with the rolling pin to apply enough pressure to get the job done well!

CHEESE N' NETTLE STUFFED CHICKEN

Cheese and Nettle Stuffed Chicken

Serves 2

Ingredients: 2 Chicken Breasts

25g Fresh Nettles

55g Soft Cheese

20g Cheddar

1 Tbs Mayonnaise

1 Tsp Paprika and Garlic Powder

25g Butter

Method:

Preheat the oven to 180c (fan assisted)

Place the fresh nettles in a small bowl and use scissors to roughly chop up the leaves. Add the soft cheese, grated cheddar (or whichever you have at home), mayonnaise, spices and combine. You can add salt and pepper to taste, or just eyeball it.

Slice down the side of each chicken breast creating a pocket, and divide the mixture evenly into both.

Over a medium heat, melt the butter in a skillet. When hot, brown the chicken each side for 3-4 minutes. As the chicken cooks on one side you can season the other side with additional salt, pepper and nettle powder before flipping and repeating the process on the other side. Transfer to the oven to cook for a further 20-25 minutes or until the chicken is cooked through.

Alternatively, if you don't own a skillet, melt the butter in a frying pan and follow the same steps before transferring to an oven proof dish for the oven.

You can skip these steps and just cook the chicken in the oven. However, I'd try it at least once browning the chicken before hand as the butter adds a deeper level of flavour to a meat which can borderline a little bland without some extra attentive preparation.

This chicken breast is very versatile in how you can serve it. Through summer it goes great on a bed of salad, or for a weekend treat you could add sweet potato fries and broccoli. Leave the breast to rest slightly before slicing and adding to a creamy pasta dish, or go all out with home cooked chips, a double whammy of a creamy mushroom sauce and wilted greens.

Hidden Nettle Bolognese

Hidden Nettle Bolognese
serves 4

Ingredients: 20g butter

1 medium onion

1 tbsp minced garlic

2 medium carrots

1 stalk of celery

500g mince (10% or higher)

1 tin of chopped tomatoes

1 bag of baby tomatoes

1 tbsp tomato puree

2 tbsp mixed herbs

3 tbsp nettle powder

200g dried pasta

Nettle wine (optional)

Method:

Melt the butter in a skillet over a medium heat, soften the onions for 5 minutes before adding the minced garlic.

Add in the carrots and celery (either diced, chopped,or - if you have picky children – grated) and cook for a further 5 minutes, trying to avoid catching on the pan.

At this stage you can quickly deglaze the pan, if you have any nettle wine dregs this is the perfect way to use that up. Add to the pan, and move the vegetables to the edges to keep softening while we add the mince.

Once the mince is browned, if there is an excess of beef fat you can add in one tablespoon of plain flour. This will soak up all that flavourful goodness and help thicken the sauce.

Incorporate the vegetables from the edges into the mince. Add the baby tomatoes, tin of chopped tomatoes, mixed herbs,tomato puree and nettle powder. Fill the empty tomato tin with water twice and add this to the pan. Now you can add the dried pasta and bring to a gentle simmer – now we're just waiting out the pasta cooking, the sauce thickening and the plum tomatoes to soften and reduce (some might need a bit of a prod and a poke to be bullied into compliance with the plan) Be careful to keep the Bolognese moving as the pasta can stick if left unattended for too long. This should take around 15-20 minutes.

If you're cooking this without children in mind, a few minutes before cooking is the perfect time to add in some fresh tops of nettles and wilt in like spinach – wild garlic would also be a tasty foraged addition if it's in season.

Plate up, and enjoy!

Parsnip, Wild Garlic and Nettle Soup

Parsnip, Wild Garlic & Nettle Soup

Ingredients: 1 Parsnip

1 large white potato

1 onion

20g butter

100g mixed weight wild garlic and fresh nettles

Vegetable stock (enough to cover vegetables)

Double cream - optional

Method:

Dice all the vegetables and sweat in a lidded pan with the butter for 20 minutes.

Cover with vegetable stock and simmer for 10 minutes.

Wilt in wild garlic and nettles.

Process in a blender (use a blender, food processor, stick blender etc) and return to a low heat to warm back up before serving with a swirl of double cream and lots of cracked black pepper.

Note: For extra foraged goodness, before blending, add in fresh or re-hydrated wood ear.

SIMPLE NETTLE PASTA SALAD

Pesto, Nettle & Feta Pasta Salad
serves 1 (good for dinner on the go)

Ingredients: 100g Pasta
3 Spring nettle heads (wilted)
A handful of Plum Tomatoes
Pesto
5 heads of Purple Dead Nettles
Feta, crumbled

Method:

Add your personal liking of pesto into the pasta.

Wilt the nettles quickly in boiled water for a minute or two (also removes the sting) and add to the bowl.

Rinse and roughly chop the purple dead nettles, adding these to the salad alongside the plum tomatoes, crumbled feta (again, to your liking – no judgement cast from me as given the opportunity I'd add half a block) and give it all a good toss (oioi) to combine.

Enjoy your incredibly pretty salad cold, or with a warmed ciabatta drizzled with olive oil and balsamic vinegar.

Parmesan and Nettle Scones

Nettle Scones
makes 8

Ingredients: 100g salted butter (cubed, room temp)

225g self raising flour

1 egg, weight made up to 120g with oat milk

1 tsp baking powder

2 tablespoons nettle powder

50g grated cheddar

20g grated parmesan

Method:

Preheat oven to 200c (fan assisted) and line a baking tray with grease proof paper.

In a large mixing bowl, tip in the flour, baking and nettle powder. Add in the butter and rub with your fingers to incorporate until it looks like breadcrumbs (and smells like heaven, lets be fair)

Make a well in the middle, and tip in the egg/milk mixture and cheddar. Work the flour in with your hands, this will be incredibly sticky going but keep at it until a rough dough comes together.

Tip the dough onto a lightly floured worktop and knead until it comes together as a soft dough.

Roll to around 1" thick, and using a 2.5" cutter (I use a glass) cut out as many scones as you can, placing on the baking tray leaving a few centimetres of space.

Bring the dough back together, kneading slightly, before rolling out again and cutting again. You should get roughly 8 scones, the last formed by hand but will be just as tasty if not the best looker.

Brush the tops with a little milk, sprinkle the parmesan over generously and bake in the oven for around 12-14 minutes.

Once cooked, leave to cool slightly before transferring to a wire rack to cool completely.

These are delicious with soup or just on their own with butter.

Nettle Preservation

Nettles are probably the bane of every gardeners life, as they make themselves known most to the year. However, when it comes to eating nettles it's the freshest of shoots that do us the most good. Once the nettles start to flower, their heads drooping with seeds, they can hinder rather than boost our health. This being said, as soon as you see them appearing in your garden around March you have many months of good nettle picking a head, so there's no rush to preserve them for the purpose of making teas. However, if you want a good powder for the year, it's best to make hay while the sun shines. Or, I suppose, best make powder while the shoots sprout.

The process does require extra equipment than the average kitchen may have. However, if you're finding your feet in the world of free food these items do have a multitude of uses and will feel essential before you know it. Of course, it's sheer common sense to consider that we, as a people, have found ways to harvest and preserve the plants of our land for generations. Ergo there is a way to do it without modern conveniences, which I'm sure you can find the infomaton on if you lean towards simply enjoying attempting to do things in line with the old ways, or are a little more budget conscious/loathe a kitchen counter full of gadgets you use once then never again (but, I don't think this will be the case here)

A dehydrator – This makes light work of drying nettles, but is also useful for preserving all fungi along with countless other herbs – and a useful way to make sure no going over fruit goes to waste.

A coffee grinder – The perfect tool for not just powdering nettles but making no end of wild powders. I'm sure, in time, you will have an abundant store of immune system boosting super-powders, as nothing will get your dandelion coffee powder finer for a brew. It's bio-hacking in its purest form.

Jars – These come freely with our grocery shopping, I have a particular sweet spot for Aldi's pesto jars as they're the perfect size for home blended spice mixes. But an old chilli sauce jar is just a fun challenge to try and fill with nettle powder while you can. Simply wash, removing the label, and sterilise in a hot oven before use. I shamelessly have a cupboard full of empty jars and happily womble them from other peoples kitchens.

Drying Nettles

Type: Fresh Nettle Tops

Equipment: Dehydrator

Method: It's best to dehydrate the nettles straight away, so plan to do this on a day you're already about the house. Collect your nettles tops from the garden or your preferred nettle patch as usual, and rinse under a running tap. Shake off any excess water.

Set your dehydrator to around 50-55c, and transfer the fresh tops to the trays. **Tip:** I find using a tea towel helps in moving the leaves around to space them out on the dehydrator trays, however the leaves do dry incredibly quickly so you don't need to be at all precious in spacing them out away from each other.

Leave for around 5 hours, rotating the trays if necessary. And you're good to go! Check through the leaves to make sure they're thoroughly dry, if not just increase the time by 30 minutes until they are. Bigger leaves, thicker stems and excess water will alter drying time.

From this point you can choose to store them as is, using them whole through the off season months in place of fresh tops in nettle tea, or add them slowly to your coffee grinder and mill to a fine powder.

Both, when dried correctly, can be stored and used for up to 18 months.

A Message from 'The Author';

I truly am a terrible rambler. At the grand age of 31 my Mum still pulls me up on my questionable grammar through texts. Although we can argue it's more her fault than mine as I didn't go out and Home Educate myself.

I really do hope I've complied these recipes in such a way that is easy to follow. I do have an awful habit of thinking I'm remarkably clever and funny, I tend to waffle on and even an edited version of my recipes seem impossible to fully strip of my mannerisms. For this, I do apologise. But equally, what's the point in not at least trying to make things a *little* bit pretty while we're here?

As mentioned in the foreword, foraging is still very new to me, so my rotation of recipes continues to grow. During the time I spent compiling the recipes for this book, I've discovered two new ways to incorporate nettles into our meals. Due to this I know once you've got to grips with a few of these recipes, and knowing your loved ones tastebuds better than me, you'll be adding you own stingy twist to meals in ways I haven't even considered yet.

And now, without a hint of cringe, thank you beyond measure for taking the time to read my recipe book. If you have any notes, questions, criticisms, or simply wish to get in touch after reading, please feel beyond welcome to reach out via email @ conkerspantry@gmail.com

Foraging courses to learn more about the feasts at our feet can be booked with my partner Henry at his ancestral woodland home in Bristol via @daggerwood_campsite on Instagram. Courses cover ways in which our woodland carpets and country hedgerows can complement our modern day diets, with obvious focus on seasonal growth. As his true foragers heart belongs to Fungi, we also host an annual Fungi Fest locally each Autumn – information to this can also be found on our Instagram.

Printed in Great Britain
by Amazon